Handmade Cards

Polly Pinder

SEARCH PRESS

First published in Great Britain 2000

Search Press Limited
Wellwood, North Farm Road,
Tunbridge Wells, Kent TN2 3DR

Text copyright © Polly Pinder 2000

Photographs by Search Press Studios
Photographs and design copyright © Search Press Ltd.
2000

ISBN 0 85532 887 8

Suppliers
If you have difficulty in obtaining any of the materials and
equipment mentioned in this book, then please visit the
Search Press website for details of suppliers:
www.searchpress.com
Alternatively, you can write to the Publishers at the
address above, for a current list of stockists, which includes
firms who operate a mail order scrvice.

The author would like to thank the following paper
suppliers for their generosity in providing many of the
handmade papers used in this book:

R. K. Burt & Company Ltd.
57 Union Street, London SE1 1SG

Falkiner Fine Papers
76 Southampton Row, London WC1B 4AR

> **Publisher's note**
> All the step-by-step photographs in this book feature
> the author, Polly Pinder, demonstrating how to
> make greetings cards. No models have been used.

Colour separation by Graphics '91 Pte Ltd, Singapore
Printed in Spain by A. G. Elkar S. Coop. 48180 Loiu (Bizkaia)

Contents

Introduction

Making cards for family and friends is absorbing, addictive and fun. How wonderful to disregard the whole world for a few hours and create a little masterpiece. The pleasure is all yours, and then the finished card is sent to someone else and the pleasure is reborn. The French have a perfect phrase for such hand-made cards – *carte à offrir* – which simply means, 'a card that is also a gift'.

The aim of this book is to present simple ideas for making cards. You can copy the examples shown, or use them as a basis for your own designs. Most of the cards have been made with no specialised equipment and relatively inexpensive materials. In fact, the most expensive part may be the card from which it is made – especially if shop-bought blanks are used. I always prefer to make my own blanks (see pages 8–9). I try to ensure that these look professional – with clean, sharp folds and edges that meet perfectly. I have also included a section on making envelopes – these can be used to great effect to enhance and complement your cards.

I show you how to make cards using a variety of man-made and natural materials – from cotton, velvet and netting to polythene, tissue paper, sea shells and sand! I have included sections on using paper, fabric and natural materials.

Start collecting things to decorate your cards. If, like me, you are a natural hoarder you will be one step ahead. Things might include any shiny, textured or unusual materials or objects that could be used to make and embellish your card. Grasses, flowers and leaves can also be gathered, dried and stored for later use. Be inventive, and you will soon discover that there is no end to the amount of objects or materials that can be used to make cards. The possibilities are limited only by your imagination.

Finally, I have included a section on lettering. You can use decorative lettering to add a personal touch to the front of your card. I have also included an alphabet guide to help you add hand-written greetings inside your finished card. Patterns for the project designs are included with the projects, and those for the variation cards can be found at the back of the book.

I hope that your beautifully crafted hand-made cards will never be discarded. They will be carefully wrapped in tissue, placed in a drawer and generations later, be discovered by someone who wonders who could have made this lovely gift.

Materials & Equipment

The materials and equipment used in this book are readily available from DIY stores, stationers, art and craft suppliers and supermarkets. You may even have many of the items in your own home.

The materials shown on these two pages are the basic ones needed for the projects in this book. This list is by no means exhaustive. As you become more creative I am certain that you will discover other materials and equipment.

The papers, fabrics and natural materials specific to each project are listed on the relevant page.

The materials required for the variation cards at the end of each project, are referred to in the captions.

CARD Ready-made blank cards are widely available. Most are made from good-quality card and are accurately folded and cut. However, they can be expensive and it may be cheaper to make your own (see pages 8–9). A wide range of **card** (12) is suitable for making your own card blanks. **Corrugated cardboard** (13) is useful for building up layers in three-dimensional cards and for making frames.

ADHESIVES I use four types of adhesive. **General purpose glue** (3) is strong and sticks almost immediately. It is excellent for securing card on to card. Petroleum-based **rubber solution glue** (1) is perfect for paper, tissue and card. It should be thinly applied to both surfaces. It will not distort your work because it contains no water. **PVA glue** (2) is a water-based adhesive. This is excellent for sticking fabric, if used sparingly, and also for dried

flora. **Double-sided sticky tape** (24) is the cleanest type of adhesive. It can be used for fabric, paper and card, but is inappropriate for materials with a very uneven surface.

Masking tape (25) This is useful for securing card and paper while cutting.

Palette knife (15) This is used for the application of rubber solution glue. Large surfaces are best dealt with using a wide, plastic spatula.

Set-square (10)   This is essential for making card blanks which must be square and have parallel sides.

Circle template (9)   This is useful for drawing circles.

Pencils (18)   Use an HB pencil for general work and a 2H for tracing. A white pencil or crayon is useful for tracing on to dark card or fabric.

Pencil eraser (7)   This is used to remove unwanted marks.

Pens (17)   There are some wonderful pens available for writing your messages: metallic gold, silver and copper; a range of fluorescent colours that can be used on pale or dark card; script felt-tipped pens; and pens with glitter suspended in glue.

Inks (8)   Bottled inks are useful for colouring certain neutral-coloured fabrics such as natural cotton, linen and hessian.

Paper punch (22)   A large range of decorative paper punches are available. The **cut-outs** (21) from paper punches have a wide range of decorative uses.

Paper crimper (11)   This transforms a piece of flat paper or card into a corrugated sheet. Different effects can be made by putting the paper/card through the crimper more than once. The quality and price of crimpers varies considerably, so think about your requirements before purchasing one. The cheaper, plastic crimpers will be fine for occasional use.

Brushes (19)   You will need a fine round brush (No. 0 or 1) for applying PVA glue to flora and other delicate materials. A medium round brush (No. 4) and a 10mm (³⁄₈in) flat brush are also useful.

SCISSORS   Good-quality scissors are always preferable. **Cuticle scissors** (6) are very useful for cutting curves. **Embroidery scissors** (5) also have their uses. Pinking shears and other **decorative scissors** (23) are not essential, but can add a little something when used with discretion.

Craft knife (16)   This is essential for cutting card and paper. Make sure you have a supply of new blades.

Rule (20)   A steel or steel-edged rule must be used when cutting with a craft knife. A measuring rule is also useful.

Cutting mat (14)   It is essential when cutting with a craft knife.

Cards and Envelopes

Greetings cards can be made from a variety of different papers and cards. Try to select colours and textures which complement the finished design.

Card is available in many different weights – heavier card is stronger and able to support more weight. Heavyweight hand-made papers are as strong as some card and are available in many beautiful colours and textures.

No matter how precise your initial measurements, the edges of a card will rarely be exactly in line with one another – unless you fold a piece of card or paper before cutting it to its final dimensions.

Most of the projects in this book use simple two-sided cards. However, three-sided cards are no more difficult to make. They have the advantage of being more stable and are hence suitable for designs which use heavier or more bulky materials. You can make cards as you need them or build up a stock of blanks.

Folding card

Most quality card can be folded in any direction, but cheaper card will produce a rough-edged fold if folded across the grain. To find out which way the grain lies, take a sample of card and make two perpendicular folds. Each fold should be parallel to two sides of the card. Compare the two folds and remember to allow for the direction of the grain when cutting the card. Always indent crease lines before folding using a dried-out ballpoint pen or an embossing tool.

Two-sided cards

1. Cut a piece of card roughly 10mm (³/₈in) larger all round than you want your finished card to be. Mark the centre with two short pencil lines. Join up the lines using a straight edge, and make an indent with a blunt instrument. The indent should be inside the completed card.

2. Fold the card inwards and run your fingers firmly along the folded edge to make a sharp crease. Erase the pencil lines.

3. Take measurements from the fold to ensure that the other edges are square and parallel. Use a steel-edged set square and a craft knife to trim the card to its final dimensions.

8

Three-sided cards

1. Cut a piece of card exactly three times the width you want your finished card to be. It should be slightly taller than the finished card. Use a pencil to draw two parallel lines to divide the card into three equal segments. Draw another line 3mm ($^1/_8$in) in from the left-hand side then trim off this edge.

2. Fold in the narrow left-hand side first – its cut edge should be just short of the second fold line. Fold in the right-hand side, turn the card over and trim the top and bottom edges using a steel-edged set-square and a craft knife.

Envelopes

You can make envelopes from a variety of materials, including gift-wrap, hand-made paper, sugar paper and used envelopes. Choose a colour to complement the colour of the card itself, or the materials embellishing the card.

Remember to make the envelope large enough for the card to slide easily in and out – allow at least 6mm ($^1/_4$in) all round as a general rule.

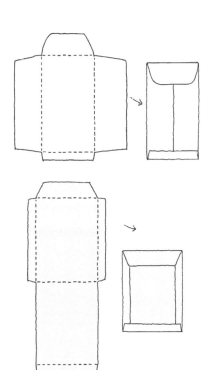

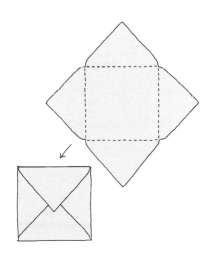

These three envelope designs can be altered to suit the size of your card. The flaps can be made narrower or wider and the top flap can be cut with decorative scissors. I always use rubber solution glue to stick the body of the envelope together, and double-sided sticky tape for the top flap.

9

Using Paper

Paper is one of man's most versatile inventions and it is eminently suitable for card-making. It can be folded, twisted, cut, torn, drawn and painted on, made into two- or three-dimensional images, and decorated in innumerable ways – the possibilities are endless. The availability of a wonderful range of good-quality machine- and hand-made papers increases our ability to produce exciting, original work. In particular, some of the hand-made papers are truly beautiful. Many are rich in colour and texture, some with interwoven natural materials, others that sparkle and shimmer as light catches their surfaces.

Some hand-made papers may appear expensive, but as greetings cards are usually small, the cost per card is relatively inexpensive. You can reduce your costs by being very careful when cutting out, and saving all 'scraps' for future use.

If you are a hoarder you can reduce your expenditure on materials considerably. Start recycling paper and card. Wrappings and packaging are the most obvious. Scrutinise the tea-bag box – could that silver lining be paper-punched and used to decorate an anniversary card? Could that chocolate wrapping be scrunched up and made into a twinkling star? The flowers on the giftwrap from last year's birthday present might be just perfect for your aunt's ninetieth birthday card! Used postage stamps can be transformed into spectacular designs and junk mail has many possibilities. Kitchen towel, napkins and doilies all add interesting textures to a design. Even cardboard boxes can be utilised to make frames and to build up layers for three-dimensional cards.

Be my Valentine

USING A TORN PAPER DESIGN

Tearing paper may at first seem an easier option than cutting, but a controlled tear sometimes takes a little practice. This simple valentine design is an ideal starting point.

Tearing the square frame for the front of the card is made easy by indenting and then folding each straight edge. The heart shapes are first drawn lightly and then torn.

I have used red gummed paper with a white backing to make the decorative heart and stripes. When this paper is torn, the red surface is pulled away from the backing to leave one side of the tear red and the other white. Practice carefully tearing the paper into little strips before you attempt the project.

You will need

A two-sided card made from red sugar paper, folded size: 140 x 140mm ($5^1/_2$ x $5^1/_2$in)

Red gummed paper, with white backing

Red sugar paper

White corrugated paper

Full-size pattern (the two small hearts can be used for a matching envelope)

Tearing paper

The grain of paper has an effect on the way paper reacts to tearing. If you tear in the same direction as the grain, the resulting edge will be fairly smooth; tearing across the grain creates a more ragged edge. To find out which way the grain lies, take a sample of paper and make two perpendicular tears. Each tear should be parallel to two sides of the card. Compare the difference between the two tears.

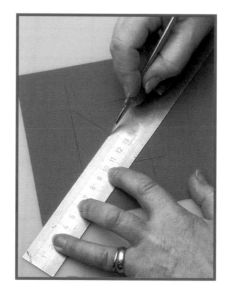

1. Open the card and draw a 60mm ($2^3/_8$in) square in the centre of the left-hand side. Indent the square using a straight edge and a blunt instrument, then cut two diagonals, corner to corner.

2. Fold each triangular section along its indented line. Carefully remove each section by tearing towards you.

3. Tear six strips, 10mm (³⁄₈in) wide, from the red gummed paper. Tear each strip towards you so that each has one white and one red edge.

4. Stick the strips across opposite corners of the front of the card. Fold the ends neatly over on to the back of the card and stick them down. Cut them off where they cross the centre-fold.

5. Cut a piece of corrugated paper to fit inside the card and cut small diagonals across the corners. Use double-sided sticky tape to attach it.

6. Trace the largest heart on to the red sugar paper then carefully tear it out. Erase any pencil marks. Repeat with the second largest heart on gummed paper, tearing it towards you to leave a fine white edge.

7. Use general purpose glue to stick the sugar paper heart on to the corrugated paper, then stick the gummed heart on top.

The finished card
140 x 140mm (5¹/₂ x 5¹/₂in)

Snow Scene
195 x 95mm (7³/₄ x 3³/₄in)
Kitchen towel and toilet paper are layered with
strips of writing paper. The sky is made from tissue
paper and stamped with a snowflake design.

Sunflower
90 x 90mm (3¹/₂ x 3¹/₂in)
The tissue for the petal was first
stuck on to ordinary writing paper,
then torn to give a white edge. The
flower centre is the crumpled lining
from a cigarette
packet.

Christmas Tree
90 x 120mm (3¹/₂ x 4³/₄in)
The branches are pieces of tissue and the
decorations are rolled crepe paper. The pot is
torn packaging indented with a dried-out
ballpoint pen.

15

Japanese Tree

USING A CUT PAPER DESIGN

Making this beautiful Japanese-inspired design involves cutting intricate shapes from card, which may take a little practice. Swivel-headed craft knifes are available for this purpose but I find them more difficult to control than normal knives.

Sometimes it helps to move the position of the card in conjunction with the knife. Use a new blade and practice on a scrap piece of card, trying to keep the blade as upright as possible. Compare this technique to holding the card still and only moving the knife. You may find that using a combination of both techniques will work best.

Before you start make a pencil tracing of the design. Turn the tracing paper face down over the outside, middle section of the card and draw over the traced image to transfer it to the card. Remove and discard the tracing.

Cutting paper

No matter how carefully you cut a straight line with a knife and rule, you will often find that the edge of the card has crinkled or risen up slightly. This is because the knife has dragged the card fibres. To resolve the problem, run the side of your thumb nail along the edge, in the opposite direction to the cut and this will flatten the fibres again. (Machine-made cards are cut by plunging the blade vertically into the card, which produces a good clean edge.)

You will need

A three-sided card made from textured paper, folded size:
100 x 185mm (4 x 7¼in)
Hand-made red glitter paper

Full-size pattern

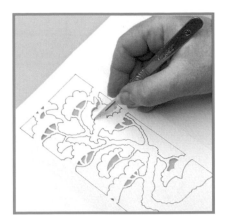

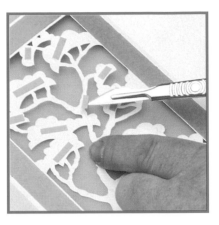

1. Place the card on a cutting mat and cut out all the background shapes (shown shaded on the pattern). Use a sharp blade and start cutting the smallest pieces first. Use a steel rule as a guide when cutting the straight sides of the image.

2. Use a soft eraser to gently remove any pencil marks. Hold down the cut image with your other hand to prevent any of the narrow pieces from breaking.

3. Turn the card over. Position strips of double-sided sticky tape round the edge of the image. Then place small pieces of tape at intervals along the trunk and foliage of the tree. Leave the backing on for the moment.

4. Apply a thin film of rubber solution glue to the back of the red glitter paper and to the inside of the left-hand section of the card. Stick the paper to the card.

5. Remove the backing from the pieces of double-sided sticky tape. Turn the card over and, working from the fold, carefully press the cut-out design on to the red glitter paper.

The finished card
100 x 185mm (4 x 7¹/₄in)

Snow Scene
75 x 125mm (3 x 5in)
The textured card used for these trees was originally a file, too good to be used for storing paper!

Good Luck
90 x 90mm (3¹/₂ x 3¹/₂in)
Chocolate wrapping creates a sparkle round this good luck card. The horse shoes were cut from a tea-bag box and the nail holes indented using a dried-up ballpoint pen.

Dancing Dollies
170 x 90mm (6³/₄ x 3¹/₂in)
The traditional method of folding and cutting a single image, then unfolding was used for these dolls. The striped background and stars were cut from the designs found inside envelopes.

Patchwork Landscape

USING A THREE-DIMENSIONAL DESIGN

This three-dimensional card is fixed in place so that none of the parts move when the card is opened. Each layer is built up a little higher than the previous one using small pieces of card to raise the layers. Polystyrene foam or sponge work equally well.

I used stiff corrugated packing for the frame and cut it in one piece, on the bias, with the grooves crossing the frame diagonally. This packing comes in two types, single- and double-corrugated, and in a variety of thicknesses, allowing some flexibility with the depth of your design.

You will need

A two-sided white card, folded size:
100 x 100mm (4 x 4in)

Tissue paper – blue for the sky, yellow for clouds and red for the sun

Corrugated card – brown for the tree trunks and fawn, brown and orange for the fields

Textured paper – green for the foliage and yellow for the frame

Double-corrugated cardboard

White card

1. Draw a 6mm (¼in) border round the edges of the front of the card.

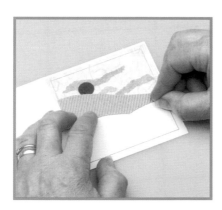

2. Trace and cut out all the shapes then use rubber solution glue to stick the sky, clouds and sun on to the front of the card. Use PVA glue for the horizon.

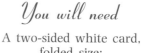

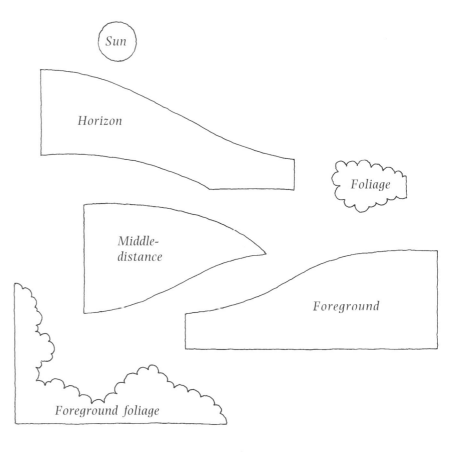

Sun

Horizon

Foliage

Middle-distance

Foreground

Foreground foliage

Enlarge these images by 133% for full-size patterns

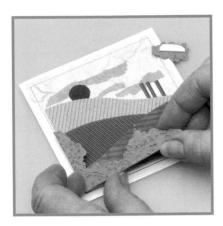

3. Cut tree trunks from brown corrugated cardboard, then use PVA glue to stick them on to the horizon. Use small pieces of card fixed to the back of the other shapes to build up the successive layers of the landscape, as shown.

4. Cut a 100mm (4in) square from double-corrugated cardboard, with the corrugations running diagonally. Cut an 88mm (3½in) square from the inside to leave a 6mm (¼in) border all round.

5. Cut four thin strips of white card the same width as the thickness of the corrugated cardboard. Use PVA glue to stick the strips neatly round the edges of the outer frame.

6. Cut a 104mm (4⅛in) square, with a 10mm (⅜in) border from the yellow textured paper. Use PVA glue to stick the corrugated frame on to the back of it, leaving an equal overlap (see insert).

7. Check that the frame fits comfortably over the three-dimensional image. Trim off any little pieces that may be in the way, then stick the frame to the card using general purpose glue.

The finished card
100 x 100mm (4 x 4in)

Wedding Anniversary
90 x 90mm (3¹/₂ x 3¹/₂in)
Various layers were stuck to the crumpled silver tissue paper background. First, a paper doily; then, a circle of thick card covered with blue cellophane; next, a circle of open-weave paper; and finally a ring made from twisted paper, painted silver.

Balloon
90 x 210mm (3¹/₂x 8¹/₄in)
This balloon, cut from crumpled tissue and mounted on to thin card, was decorated with gummed paper shapes bought from a craft shop. The clouds were cut from hand-made paper.

Apples
110 x 90mm (4¹/₄ x 3¹/₂in)
The textured pattern on the fruit bowl was achieved by putting the card through a paper crimper twice. I used a decorative paper punch to cut the apples, then painted the stalks gold.

Using Fabric

Fabric has great potential when it comes to making cards. It also adds another dimension when used in conjunction with the exciting hand-made papers that are now available. Both natural and synthetic fabrics can be used – each has different qualities which can enhance a design. Natural fabrics often come in natural shades such as fawns, creams and greys. Cards made using these subtle colours will produce a very different effect to those made with brightly-coloured, shimmering synthetics.

Most of us will have an old box somewhere in the house containing scraps of fabric – left-overs from a sewing project; old garments now considered unfashionable but too good to discard; denim jean legs which were cut off to make a pair of shorts; a beautiful silk shirt, unwearable because of one small stubborn stain on the front. Now these can all be put to good use.

If you do not have a store of fabric, and need to buy some, choose remnants and off-cuts from the market – these are usually much cheaper than those available in department stores. Charity shops and jumble sales can also provide cheap but wonderful fabrics in the form of silk scarves, satin blouses, hessian bags and even lace underwear!

A pair of good-quality, medium-sized, sharp scissors is essential. Cutting tiny pieces of fabric will be much easier if you also have a pair of small, sharp embroidery scissors. Pinking shears are useful for decorative purposes. Fancy-edged scissors are perfect for paper and thin card, but cannot cope with material.

Poppy Field

USING NATURAL FABRICS

Natural fabrics fray beautifully. Linen and similar open-weave materials are particularly effective, but the fraying (in most cases) should be controlled so as to look natural.

For this design I exaggerated the fraying of the linen to represent long grass. The red silk frays slightly when cutting out the petals, to give the poppies a soft-edged, natural look. The black cotton velvet used for the poppy centres also frays to give more texture.

I tend to use hand-made papers in conjunction with fabrics, but even inexpensive plain card can be used to produce very attractive results. For this example, I used a basic plain white card with a textured hand-made paper frame to complement the design.

You will need

A two-sided white card, folded size:
100 x 190 mm (4 x 7½in)

Textured hand-made paper, 100 x 190mm (4 x 7½in)

Pale blue fine-weave cotton, 80 x 160mm (3⅛ x 6¼in)

Natural-coloured linen, 80 x 110mm (3⅛ x 4¼in)

Small piece of red silk

Black cotton velvet

Polythene bag

Yellow and green ink

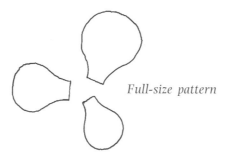

Full-size pattern

1. Use two narrow strips of double-sided sticky tape to stick the pale blue fine-weave cotton to the front of the card. Allow an even border all round.

2. Cut a wavy line across the top of the piece of linen.

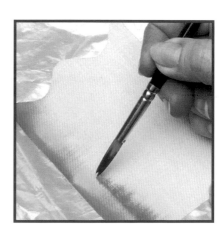

3. Wet the fabric then squeeze out the excess water. Lay the damp linen on a polythene bag. Brush vertical stripes of yellow and green inks on to the fabric, allowing the colours to blend. Leave to dry.

26

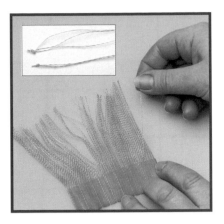

4. Use the pattern as a guide to cut out eight large, four medium and four small petals from a piece of red silk. Scrunch each petal into a ball, and then release to give a crumpled effect (see insert).

5. Pull away the horizontal weft fibres from the wavy edge of the linen. Stop 30mm (1¼in) from the lower edge.

6. Make vertical lines in the unfrayed section of the fabric by pulling out nine groups of three adjacent warp threads. Knot three strands together at one end to make a stem, then make another (see insert).

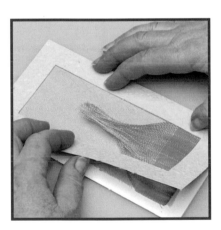

7. Stick the unfrayed section of the linen grass to the card with double-sided sticky tape. Cut the textured hand-made paper to create a border, 20mm (¾in) wide at the top and sides and 25mm (1in) at the bottom. Gather the warp threads of the frayed section as shown and use double-sided sticky tape to stick the frame in position.

8. Spread the warp threads apart and use small blobs of PVA glue to stick the stems and petals in position. Position the petals so that two of the poppies sit over the edge of the frame.

9. Finally, cut the poppy centres from a piece of black cotton velvet, allowing each to fray a little. Stick them into position using PVA glue.

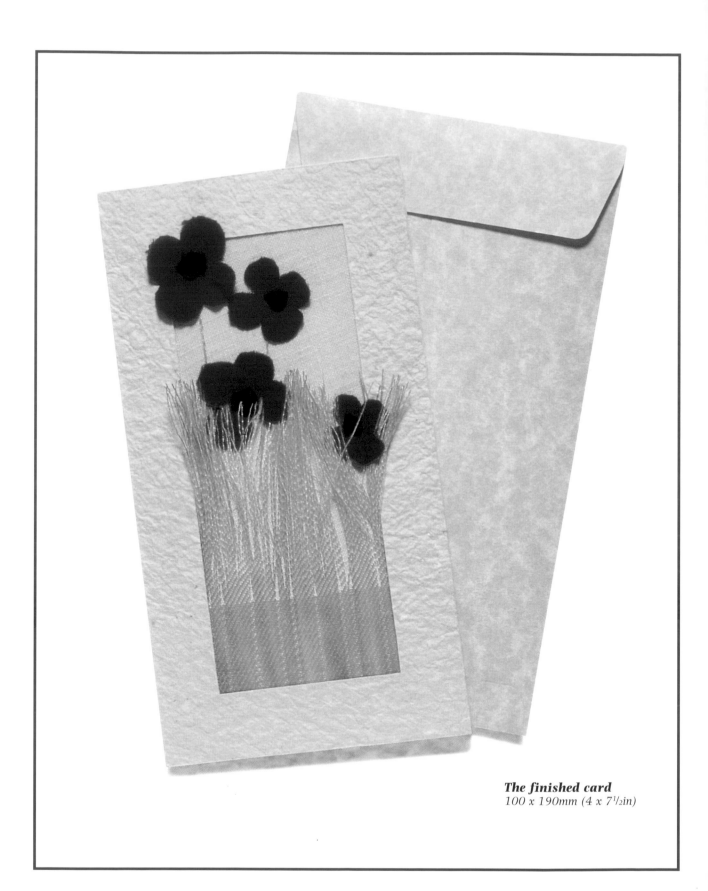

The finished card
100 x 190mm (4 x 7¹/₂in)

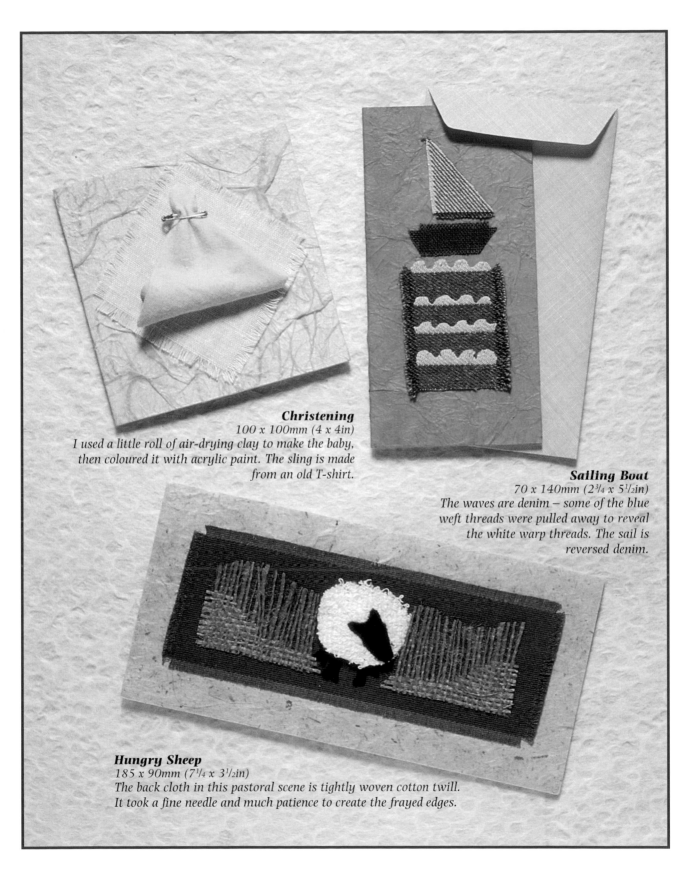

Christening
100 x 100mm (4 x 4in)
I used a little roll of air-drying clay to make the baby,
then coloured it with acrylic paint. The sling is made
from an old T-shirt.

Sailing Bout
70 x 140mm (2³/₄ x 5¹/₂in)
The waves are denim – some of the blue
weft threads were pulled away to reveal
the white warp threads. The sail is
reversed denim.

Hungry Sheep
185 x 90mm (7¹/₄ x 3¹/₂in)
The back cloth in this pastoral scene is tightly woven cotton twill.
It took a fine needle and much patience to create the frayed edges.

Jazzy Giraffe

USING SYNTHETIC FABRICS

Many synthetic fabrics have shiny surfaces which can add an interesting element of fantasy to the images cut from them. Old evening wear is perfect. I found some black and shimmering gold fabric which was ideal for making the giraffe in this project.

Frayed synthetic fabrics are often not very attractive. I overcome the problem by placing double-sided sticky tape on to the back of the fabric before cutting. In this project, the material I used for the giraffe was not rigid enough to work with, so I backed it on to a piece of black cartridge paper. This made it much easier to handle when tracing and cutting the image

You will need

A three-sided card made from textured hand-made paper, folded size:
110 x 200mm (4¼ x 8in)

Black cartridge paper,
100 x 190mm (4 x 7½in)

Pale blue fabric,
100 x 190mm (4 x 7½in)

Small piece of green netting

Small piece of yellow fabric

Black and gold fabric,
100 x 190mm (4 x 7½in)

Short length of black cord

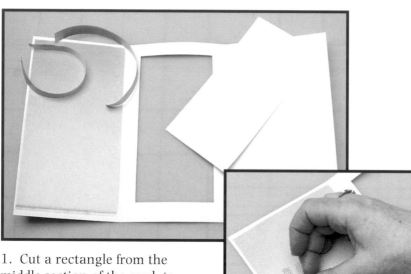

1. Cut a rectangle from the middle section of the card, to leave a 15mm (⁵/₈in) border at the top and sides, and 20mm (³/₄in) at the bottom. Use two narrow strips of double-sided sticky tape to stick the pale blue fabric to the inside of the left-hand section.

2. Cut six narrow strips of green netting; three to represent the land and three for the tree trunks. Use small pieces of double-sided sticky tape to stick these strips to the blue fabric. The frame should cover all the pieces of tape, except those at the top of the trunks.

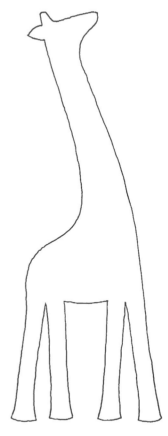

Full-size pattern

3. Cut four wavy-edged 40mm (1½in) diameter circles of netting. Brush the centre of each circle with PVA glue and stick them over the top of the tree trunks. Arrange them so that they are not quite aligned with each other.

4. Run a trail of general purpose glue round the edge of the frame, then fold and press the left-hand section firmly over the opening.

5. Stick a piece of double-sided sticky tape to the back of the yellow fabric. Draw a circle on the backing then cut it out to make the sun. Carefully remove the backing and stick the sun on to the sky.

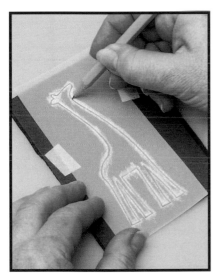

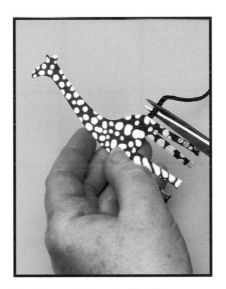

6. Cover the back of the black and gold fabric with double-sided sticky tape. Remove the backing then stick the fabric on to a piece of black cartridge paper. Make a tracing of the giraffe template, rub the back of the tracing with a white pencil or crayon, then transfer the image on to the black cartridge paper.

7. Cut out the giraffe. Use a short length of black cord to make the giraffe's tail. Stick it in place using a small piece of double-sided sticky tape, then trim to size.

8. Finally, use general purpose glue to stick the giraffe on to the card.

The finished card
110 x 200mm (4¹/₄ x 8in)

Christmas Trees

80 x 120mm (3¹/₄ x 4³/₄in)
The strands of the metallic netting used for this card were relatively thick, so it was possible to apply thin trails of PVA glue to stick the netting to the background fabric.

Fish

110 x 110mm (4¹/₄ x 4¹/₄in)
The corrugated background for this card was produced by sticking textured tissue paper on to plain writing paper, then putting it through a paper crimper.

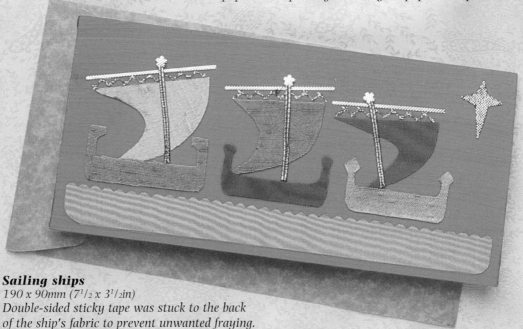

Sailing ships

190 x 90mm (7¹/₂ x 3¹/₂in)
Double-sided sticky tape was stuck to the back of the ship's fabric to prevent unwanted fraying.

Using Natural Materials

Hand-made cards can look very effective when embellished with dried flora and natural objects. The materials used for the cards in this chapter include just a few of the many that can be utilised for your cards.

Use your imagination. Onion skins lose their pungent aroma after pressing and they have wonderful variations of colour – from pale and translucent cinnamon, to rich and opaque burnt orange. Patterns could be formed by varying the direction of their fine, straight veins, or a simple mosaic could be cut from them.

An old straw hat, too battered to wear but too beautifully woven to throw away, could come in useful. A piece cut from the crown would make a stunning vase, which in turn could be filled with tiny, pressed flower buds and delicate leaves, then mounted on hand-made paper.

Design concepts are best kept simple, and remember that unless your card is to be hand-delivered or boxed, it will have to go through the rigours of the normal posting system. Envelopes are surprisingly strong and protective, but there is a limit to their ability to prevent your work of art from being damaged. Do not be afraid of using three-dimensional objects, but always test them out first and remember to allow for their depth when making the envelope. Finally, bear in mind balance – the card should stand upright and not fall on its face!

Conifer Trees

USING DRIED FLORA

Small pieces of conifer are used to decorate this card. The delicate, feathery appearance of each piece complements the textured tissue paper perfectly.

Dried and pressed plant material have been used for years to decorate greetings cards. There are many excellent books dedicated entirely to the subject of growing, gathering, drying and pressing plants, so here I will explain only the basic techniques.

Gather all flora on a warm, dry morning, after the dew has evaporated and before flowers begin to wilt in the heat of the sun. Flowers for drying should have most of the foliage removed from their stems. Tie them into small bunches and hang in a cool, airy room away from direct sunlight. I usually place a paper bag very loosely over the flower heads to keep out as much light as possible and to protect them from dust. Grasses, seed heads and leaf stems can all be dried in the same way.

You will need

A two-sided white card,
folded size:
95 x 195mm (3¾ x 7¾in)

Green textured tissue paper,
100 x 200mm (4 x 8in)

Mount board,
90 x 180mm (3½ x 7in)

Pale green textured tissue paper,
90 x 180mm (3½ x 7in)

Small pieces of conifer

Pressing flowers

Pressing flowers and other flora is not a difficult process. The aim is to extract all the moisture as quickly as possible so that the plant material maintains its original colour. Lay the flowers between a sheet of folded blotting paper. Place this between several layers of newspaper, cover with a flat board, and place something heavy on top – a couple of bricks or some large books for example. The best storage place is somewhere warm and dry – an airing cupboard, or next to an oven or boiler is ideal. Most flowers should be pressed in two weeks but very succulent ones will take a little longer.

Enlarge this image by 200% for a full-size pattern

36

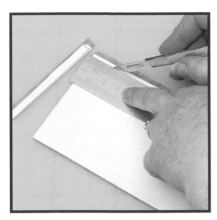

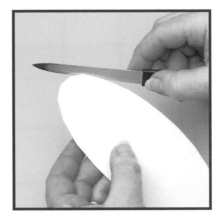

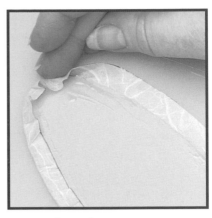

1. Apply a thin film of rubber solution glue to the green tissue paper and the front of the card. Carefully align the tissue with the folded edge of the card then smooth it into place. Leave to dry, then turn the card over and trim 5mm (¼in) off the three unfolded sides.

2. Use the template and a pair of small scissors to cut an oval out of the mount board. Use a nail file to smooth the edges.

3. Cut the pale green tissue slightly larger than the oval mount board, then use rubber solution glue to stick them together. Fold the overlap round to the back of the oval and smooth out all creases.

4. Stick the oval to the front of the card with general purpose glue, leaving a gap of 12mm (½in) at the top and sides and 18mm (¾in) at the bottom. Leave to dry. Finally, apply fine trails of PVA glue to the pieces of conifer then stick them on to the oval.

The finished card
90 x 185mm (3$\frac{1}{2}$ x 7$\frac{1}{4}$in)

Flower Buds
180 x 80mm (7 x 3¼in)
Simple arrangements are often very effective,
particularly when highly-textured hand-made
paper is included as part of the design.

Dried Flower
100 x 115mm (4 x 4½in)
A hole was cut in the middle section of a three-sided
card and a piece of mount board. The board was
then sandwiched between the left-hand and middle
sections of the card. The extra depth gives some
protection to the flower head.

Christmas Wreath
90 x 125mm (3½ x 5in)
The little berries which form part of the
wreath were cut in half and pressed
before being stuck to the card. The card
is not as delicate as it may appear and it
should cope with the rigours of the
postal system!

Ocean Scene

USING NATURAL OBJECTS

The most important thing to remember when using natural objects is balance. String, raffia, cork, loofah and tiny shells are all fairly light and should not disturb the balance of your card. However, heavier objects such as pebbles might topple the card over. Test the balance by attaching the object to a card using a temporary adhesive. Compromise if necessary, by reducing the number or weight of your objects.

   You need not worry about balance when making this card, providing you choose fairly lightweight sea shells. However, you should be aware of the size of the shells you are using and adjust the depth of the frame accordingly.

You will need

A two-sided card made from textured hand-made paper, folded size:
80 x 160mm (3 x 6in)

Aquamarine corrugated or crimpled paper

Black or dark blue mount board

Dark blue paper

Small piece of blue cellophane

Fine sand

Tiny sea shells

Sprigs of fern or conifer

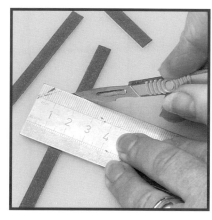

1. Draw a 30 x 70mm (1¼ x 2¾in) rectangle on the front of the card, leaving a gap of 25mm (1in) from the top and sides. Cut a piece of blue cellophane to the same size. Use rubber solution glue to stick the cellophane over the rectangle.

2. Roughly apply a thin film of rubber solution glue to the lower half of the cellophane, avoiding the edges. Sprinkle fine sand over the adhesive then leave to dry. Shake off any excess sand.

3. Cut four 7mm (¼in) wide strips of mount board – two 70mm (2¾in) long and two 30mm (1¼in) long.

4. Use PVA glue to stick the edge of the strips (coloured side innermost) round the cellophane to form a box frame.

5. Cut a long length of dark blue paper 7mm (¼in) wide and use PVA glue to stick this round the outside of the box frame. Ensure that the join is in the middle of the bottom edge.

6. Work up a design with shells and sprigs of fern or conifer. When you are happy with the arrangement, stick each piece in position – use PVA glue for the sprigs and general purpose glue for the shells.

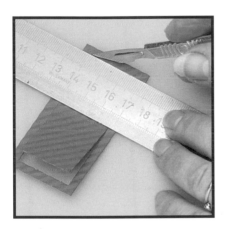

7. Cut the front of the frame from corrugated paper with outer dimensions of 36 x 76mm (1⅜ x 3in) and inner dimensions of 28 x 68mm (1⅛ x 2⅝in).

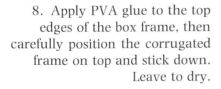

8. Apply PVA glue to the top edges of the box frame, then carefully position the corrugated frame on top and stick down. Leave to dry.

The finished card
80 x 160mm (3¹/₄ x 6¹/₄in)

Bunch of Flowers
80 x 100mm (3¼ x 4in)
*Sliced wine bottle corks, bits of
loofah and feathers from an old
feather duster were used to create
this flower arrangement.*

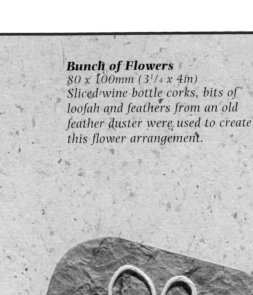

Single Flower Head
80 x 80mm (3¼ x 3¼in)
*The centre of this flower was made from
broken eggshells. They were stuck on to a
circle of double-sided sticky tape, which was
then attached to a torn circle of hand-made
tissue paper.*

Tree on a Rock
80 x 130mm (3¼ x 5in)
*I used a serrated bread knife to cut a slice of
'rock' from this natural sea sponge. The tree
is a piece of thick string, frayed at one end to
form the foliage.*

Lettering

Many splendid books have been written on the subject of lettering, but here I have included just a few examples of what is suitable for use on the front of a card. I have used a different style and technique for each letter, and they appear on a variety of hand-made papers and cards. By experimenting with different styles, techniques and materials you can create lettering to complement your design.

Gold and silver paint
Outline the letter then fill it in using a fine brush and gold and silver paint. Gold and silver pens are available but are not quite as accurate for formal lettering.

Stamped image
Shop-bought stamps can be quite expensive, but they have the advantage of being reusable. Many stamping techniques can be used to vary the image.

Cut-out textured paper
Trace the reversed letter on to the back of textured paper then carefully cut it out. This technique is easier if the paper is textured on one side only.

Embossed foil
This was the foil seal inside a tin of coffee. Cut the letter shape from a piece of thin card. Secure the foil on to a newspaper. Place the reversed letter shape on to the foil and indent the outline using a ballpoint pen.

Glitter glue
Outline the letter. Squeeze a trail of glitter glue over it, then use a fine brush to spread the glue out until the letter is filled in. Leave to dry.

Corrugated mosaic
Cut a strip of flat-backed corrugated paper, two ridges wide, into squares and triangles. Stick them, flat-side down, to your card using blobs of PVA glue.

Stencil
It is not difficult to make your own stencil. Outline a letter on to a piece of thin card and carefully cut it out. Remember to leave bridges, connecting bowls to the background.

Magazine cut-outs
Choose quality paper so that print from the reverse side does not show through. Use long-bladed scissors for cutting straight lines and cuticle scissors for curves.

Paper punch cut-outs
Decorative paper punches can be bought from craft shops. The designs are available in a wide variety of different shapes and sizes. Use tiny dabs of PVA glue to stick the cut-outs to your card.

ABCDEFGHIJKLMNO
PQRSTUVWXYZ
abcdefghijklmno
pqrstuvwxyz
1234567890

Alphabet
The message inside your card can be as short or as elaborate as you wish, but in order not to spoil the whole impression, it should be legible. Some people are fortunate enough to have beautiful hand-writing, those who have not could use this simple alphabet as a guide.

Patterns

The patterns on these two pages are for the variation cards at the end of each project. They are all reproduced full-size. If you want to make a card smaller or larger than the given dimensions you can reduce or enlarge the pattern on a photocopier.

Apples,
page 23

Hungry Sheep,
page 29

Dancing Dollies,
page 19

Snow Scene,
page 19

Fish, page 33

Sailing Boat,
page 29

Christmas Trees,
page 33

Good Luck,
page 19

Balloon, page 23

Sailing Ships, page 33

47

Index